Stop Smoking

A Comprehensive And Systematic Approach To The
Efficient Treatment Of Chronic Common Diseases

*(Strategies For Overcoming Smoking Addiction And
Achieving Long-Term Smoking Cessation)*

Dr. Donald Therrien

TABLE OF CONTENT

Nicotine Replacement Therapy: Different Approaches And Tips For A Successful Outcome 1

The Advantages And Disadvantages Of Using Each Technique, As Well As Suggestions On How To Select The Most Appropriate Method 12

Therapy For Nicotine Substitution (Nrt) 19

The Stages That Make Up The Trip 25

Returning To Good Health 30

Selecting A Method For Quitting 37

Find Yourself A Buddy With A Computer. 44

Regarding Your Ongoing Support 64

Why Do You Even Bother To Start Smoking In The First Place? 69

The Dangers Of Smoking To One's Health 84

Putting The Pieces In Place For Victory............. 90

The Easiest Way To End Your Addiction To Cigarettes 107

Becoming A Member Of Support Groups As Well As Online Communities............................... 116

People Who Try To Quit Smoking May Find It Simpler To Do So If They Follow These Suggestions. 121

The Adverse Impacts Of Cigarette Use On The Individual 138

Taking Charge Of Your Quitting Process Through The Use Of Self-Hypnosis 147

Nicotine Replacement Therapy: Different Approaches And Tips For A Successful Outcome

Nicotine replacement therapy, also known as NRT, is a potentially helpful method for helping people kick their smoking habit. Nicotine replacement therapy (NRT) is a form of smoking cessation treatment that delivers nicotine to the body while avoiding the inhalation of the toxic chemicals that are found in cigarette smoke. The following are some possibilities for NRT as well as some successful strategies:

Nicotine gum is a product that can be purchased without a prescription and is available in a wide variety of flavors and intensities. Chew the gum slowly until you get a tingling feeling, and then "park" it between your cheek and gum to allow the nicotine to be absorbed into your system.

Nicotine patch: Nicotine patches are another option that may be purchased without a prescription and deliver a consistent amount of nicotine to the user throughout the day. Put the patch on an area of your skin that is clean and dry, and change it out every day.

Nicotine lozenge Nicotine lozenges are small chewy candies that dissolve in the mouth and deliver a measured amount of nicotine. Use them in the manner specified, which most of the time involves placing them in the mouth and allowing them to dissolve gradually.

Nicotine inhaler: A nicotine inhaler is a device that vaporizes nicotine and distributes it to the user, mimicking the experience of smoking. The inhaler needs to be obtained with a prescription and used in the manner specified in the manual.

Take into consideration the following methods in order to have the most success with NRT:

Employ NRT in the manner specified: You should either carry out the steps stated on the product's packaging or carry out the steps outlined by your healthcare professional. Never use more nicotine replacement therapy (NRT) than is recommended, and never use it for longer than is specified.

lower your use of NRT gradually: Over the course of time, progressively lower the amount of NRT you use until you no longer require it. You may experience less withdrawal symptoms and less cravings if you do this.

Integrate NRT with the following other strategies: Be patient and persistent: quitting smoking is a process, and it may take some time before you start to notice effects. NRT is most effective when used in tandem with other quit smoking treatments, such as counseling or support groups. Continue to show dedication to achieving your goal, and be patient with yourself along the way.

Utilize a mixture of the following NRT products: Combining many different kinds of nicotine replacement therapy products, such as wearing a patch and chewing gum at the same time, using a lozenge and an inhaler, or using a patch, gum, and inhaler together, can assist manage cravings throughout the day and give more effective relief.

Talk to your doctor or other healthcare professional about: It is essential to have a conversation with your primary care physician prior to using NRT, particularly if you have any preexisting medical conditions or take any drugs. Your healthcare physician will be able to assist you in determining the NRT method and dosage that will work best for you.

It is important to refrain from smoking when using NRT because doing so can raise the likelihood of experiencing adverse effects and an overdose of nicotine. It is essential that you abstain from smoking when using medicines that contain NRT.

Steer clear of alcoholic beverages and caffeine-containing beverages because both of these substances can intensify the effects of nicotine and may cause NRT to become less effective. While using NRT, it is advised to abstain from or severely limit use of alcohol and caffeine.

Be aware of the possibility of adverse reactions: the use of NRT may result in adverse reactions such as nausea, dizziness, and headaches. Be aware of these possible adverse effects, and consult your healthcare practitioner if any of these symptoms become severe or continue for an extended period of time.

Maintain your commitment and motivation: The process of stopping smoking is difficult, but maintaining your motivation and dedication to your objective can assist you in overcoming challenges and achieving your goal of quitting smoking. Keep a positive attitude and a dogged determination, and center your thoughts on the advantages of quitting smoking, such as an improvement in health and cost savings.

Using nicotine replacement therapy (NRT) products can be an effective tool to help someone quit smoking; however, it is important to note that using these products is only one aspect of the road to quit smoking. It is possible to boost the likelihood of success by using NRT in conjunction with other methods, including as therapy, support groups, and adjustments to one's way of life. It is possible to kick the habit of smoking for good and reap the benefits of living a life free of tobacco use if one has access to the resources and support necessary to do so.

20 EFFECTIVE METHODS FOR PREVENTING SMOKING AMONG STUDENTS

1. Decide When You Will Quit Smoking: The first step is to decide when you will quit smoking. This not only provides you with a particular goal but also makes it possible for you to mentally prepare for the transition. It provides you with a solid foundation upon which to build your path away from smoking.

2. Look for Support Speak with people you know who can assist you in quitting, such as friends, family, or members of a support group. They have the ability to inspire you, ensure that you remain accountable, and offer guidance. If you have their support, your chances of being successful will go up significantly.

3. Recognize your smoking triggers, such as the circumstances, feelings, or persons that set off your cravings for a cigarette. You will be able to more

effectively avoid or deal with triggers if you first recognize them and then build ways to deal with them. This self-awareness enables you to maintain control of the situation.

4. Substitute smoking with healthy behaviors, such as participating in activities that divert your attention from the want to smoke, such as going for a run, pursuing a hobby, or spending time with people who do not smoke. Positive alternatives to tobacco use include engaging in healthy behaviors.

5. Look for Other Options: Consider using nicotine replacement therapy items (such as patches or gum) or investigating non-nicotine options, such as herbal cigarettes. Choosing one of these alternatives may assist you in lowering your dependence on nicotine over time.

6. Modify Your Surroundings: If you smoke, don't do it at your house or

anywhere else you frequent. Clean up the area and get rid of any smoking equipment to make the environment less tempting. Your resolve to give up smoking will be bolstered if you make the surrounding area smoke-free.

7. Get an education: Educate yourself on the negative effects of smoking on your health as well as the positive effects of stopping smoking. It might help to enhance your drive to quit smoking if you are aware of the harmful effects smoking has on your body as well as the good changes that occur when you stop smoking.

8. Picture yourself succeeding: Picture yourself succeeding in quitting smoking and reaping the benefits of doing so, such as improved health, more energy, and financial savings. During difficult times, it might be helpful to strengthen your determination by seeing yourself succeeding.

9. Engage in stress management practices, such as developing good coping mechanisms for stress, such as exercising, practicing deep breathing, meditating, or participating in other activities that are calming. Because stress can act as a catalyst for starting a smoking habit, finding healthy strategies to manage stress is critical.

10. Maintain Adequate Hydration: Consuming a sufficient amount of water might assist in the removal of toxins from the body and lessen the intensity of cravings. In addition, maintaining a healthy level of hydration is beneficial to one's general health.

The Advantages And Disadvantages Of Using Each Technique, As Well As Suggestions On How To Select The Most Appropriate Method

Every possible method of quitting has both advantages and disadvantages. The following is a summary of the most common methods for quitting, followed by some helpful hints for selecting the most appropriate approach:

1. Quitting "cold turkey" has potential benefits, including being cost-free and easier to do if you have a strong support system and enough of determination.

The withdrawal symptoms that accompany a "cold turkey" approach to quitting can be harsh and tricky to manage when you're on your own. This might make it difficult to maintain the change.

It is important to have a strong support network in place and effective coping methods for cravings and withdrawal symptoms if you are considering of quitting smoking cold turkey. This piece of advice comes from the American Cancer Society.

2. Nicotine replacement therapy benefits It is possible that this treatment will assist in the management of cravings and withdrawal symptoms.

Negative aspects include the potential for adverse consequences in certain individuals, as well as the high cost of nicotine replacement therapy.

It is recommended that you consult with a trained medical practitioner regarding the viability of nicotine replacement therapy for you as well as the optimal method of treatment. It is absolutely necessary to participate in nicotine replacement treatment and to maintain the dose that has been prescribed to you in order to successfully quit smoking.

3. The Benefits of Medication One potential benefit of medication is that it

can help control withdrawal symptoms and reduce cravings.

Drugs might not be safe or effective for everyone, and they might also have unwanted side effects.

It is recommended to consult a medical expert regarding the appropriateness of any medication as well as the selection of the optimal medication to take. Utilizing therapy and maintaining a dose that is consistent with what has been recommended is an essential component of a comprehensive quitting approach.

4. The Pros of Counseling: Counseling can aid people in developing effective coping mechanisms and in controlling the factors that cause stress.

Con: Attending counseling sessions can be an expensive and time-consuming commitment.

Take into consideration attending treatment as a component of an all-encompassing plan for quitting. Find a therapist who has experience helping individuals quit smoking and who can provide support and guidance while you work through the process of quitting smoking.

5. Benefits of support systems Support groups may give a person a sense of belonging and provide encouragement when they are quitting smoking.

Con: Support groups might not be the best option for everyone, and some individuals could feel that participating in them is too overwhelming.

As part of an all-encompassing strategy to quit smoking, you might want to think about joining a support group. Find a group that can meet your needs and work around your schedule while also providing an environment that is kind and inclusive of everyone.

6. Advantages of Complementary and Alternative Therapies: Some people find

that using alternative treatments such as hypnotherapy or acupuncture helps them better manage their stress levels and their appetites for unhealthy foods.

Alternative treatments might not be supported by scientific research, and they might not be beneficial to everyone who tries them.

Advice: If you are thinking about attempting an alternative treatment, you should first consult with your primary care physician to ensure that it is both safe and effective.

7. The Advantages of Physical Activity: Exercising on a regular basis may assist in the reduction of cravings, the management of stress and anxiety, and the improvement of general health and well-being.

Negatives: Exercising might not be for everyone, and it might take some time to see results.

It is recommended that you think about incorporating exercise into your approach for quitting smoking in order to alleviate stress and improve your overall health. Your workout program should be gradually improved over time, but you should begin with more manageable goals.

It may take some experimentation to determine which way of quitting smoking is most effective. It is essential to keep your motivation up, look for support, and continue to be dedicated to the process of quitting smoking even if you are having difficulty.

Therapy For Nicotine Substitution (Nrt)

Nicotine replacement therapy, also known as NRT, is a tried-and-true method that has been shown to successfully help people quit smoking. Nicotine replacement therapy (NRT) entails using products that contain nicotine in order to gradually lessen one's dependence on nicotine, so making the process of quitting more tolerable. In this article, we will discuss the complexities of NRT, its benefits, and the ways in which it may be able to support you on your journey toward quitting smoking.

Acquiring Knowledge of the Nicotine Replacement Therapy

Nicotine replacement therapy (NRT) is quitting smoking by using nicotine-containing products that deliver controlled levels of nicotine to the body. By providing a steady supply of nicotine, nicotine replacement therapy (NRT) helps alleviate withdrawal symptoms and cravings, which in turn makes the process of quitting smoking easier to bear.

Forms of Natural Reproductive Technology Natural reproductive technology (NRT) is available in a variety of formats, allowing you to choose the option that best suits your interests and requirements:

- Gum with Nicotine: Nicotine is released when gum is chewed, providing oral stimulation and aiding in the control of cravings.

Nicotine patches are adhesive strips that are placed on the skin to deliver a steady amount of nicotine at regular intervals throughout the day.

Nicotine Lozenges: Nicotine lozenges dissolve in the mouth, releasing nicotine in a steady stream and providing respite from urges to smoke.

- Nicotine Nasal Spray: This form of nicotine replacement therapy (NRT) is administered in the form of a nasal spray and provides almost instantaneous relief from the urge to smoke.

Nicotine inhalers: Nicotine inhalers mimic the motion of smoking by simulating the hand-to-mouth action, and they deliver nicotine in a vaporized form.

Advantages of NRT There are a number of advantages to using NRT, all of which have the potential to increase your chances of quitting smoking successfully:

Reduced Withdrawal Symptoms: Nicotine replacement therapy (NRT) assists in the management of withdrawal symptoms including as irritability, anxiety, and changes in mood, which makes the process of quitting smoking more manageable.

Weaning Off Nicotine: Nicotine replacement therapy (NRT) gives users the ability to progressively reduce the amount of nicotine they take in over time, making it easier to quit using nicotine altogether.

Enhanced Probabilities of Success: According to a number of studies, using a NRT product increases the likelihood of successfully quitting smoking in comparison to quitting on your own without any support.

Flexibility and Command: Because NRT offers a range of treatment options, you'll be able to select the modality that's most suitable for your lifestyle and preferences.

Individualized Treatment: Nicotine replacement therapy (NRT) can be tailored to meet your specific needs, and there is a wide variety of dosages and treatment plans to choose from.

Combining non-pharmacologic treatments (NRT) with behavioral strategies

It's possible that combining NRT with behavioral techniques will make it more effective. The process of nicotine replacement therapy is complemented by behavioral strategies that address the psychological aspects of addiction. These techniques include the identification of triggers, the formulation of goals, and the development of coping mechanisms.

Obtaining the Opinion of a Qualified Healthcare Professional

It is absolutely necessary to consult a medical professional before beginning to use NRT, and this is especially the case if you have any underlying health concerns. They are able to guide you in selecting the most appropriate nicotine replacement therapy (NRT) product, dose, and duration in light of your specific circumstances.

Nicotine replacement therapy, also known as NRT, is an extremely helpful tool on the path to quitting smoking. Nicotine replacement therapy (NRT) helps lessen withdrawal symptoms and cravings by delivering nicotine in controlled doses. This makes the process of quitting smoking easier to bear. When combined with behavioral techniques and the guidance of an expert, nicotine replacement therapy (NRT) may significantly improve your chances of beating nicotine addiction and living a life that is free of cigarettes and full of health benefits.

The Stages That Make Up The Trip

There are 4 steps in the smoke discharge procedure. The awareness one comes first. When discussing health issues, the smoker becomes hostile. Confirm? It is pointless to keep saying things you already know, such "It gives you cancer," "You get drunk," "Smoking causes impotence." It can be more of a speaker outburst than a danger to the smoker. However, the first stage is to undercut, debunk, and expose the smoker's false views while introducing the proper perspective on the issue of smoking. Without actually attacking, but by involving the smoker in the process and forcing him to speak for himself. The smoker is aware of his problem, and if given the best opportunity to be truthful with himself, he will genuinely admit it while preparing to listen. On the other hand, it will be over if he is judged.

What comes next after one has understood and recognized the issue to oneself? The next phase is the motivation. People will occasionally inform me that they realize it is foolish for them to continue smoking and that they don't have to. However, they either keep doing them or cease the exercises. Why? The reason being that they lack the motivation and drive to persevere through the challenges and commit themselves to following the instructions.Understanding alone won't help you improve; you also need the correct enthusiasm. It's crucial to be highly motivated to take action. Many people resume smoking when they experience negative emotions. Consider this a coincidence, do you? They lack energy, so no. They withdraw and go back to the beginning. What happens next once the drive has been found? Action! doing something and keep doing it. submitting numerous applications. focusing on the mental, emotional, and behavioral components. And last, reconditioning to replace the unhealthy and fruitless cigarette-centeredbehaviors with a new wellness habit.

Phases are described.

Knowledge and awareness are distinct concepts that are sometimes misconstrued. With regard to "clichés" and limiting views about smoking, change, and one's possibilities, awareness will be characterized by a series of reasoning, arguments, and diverse perspectives. You will discover how to produce energy, reduce negativity, and generate and sustain motivation during the motivation phase. You'll learn what motivates you to perform at your best. During the action phase, you will both start doing new things that may be extremely helpful and separate from people you have been accustomed to up to that point. You won't always be convinced of the value and efficacy of what I want you to do; some requests will appear bizarre and unrealistic, and by completing them, you might feel foolish. I could care less. The fact that they engage you in order to function is crucial. Better still if they are unusual; this indicates that they would benefit more from a change in the direction of the unknown. If they don't strike you as strange, you probably already know about them and have perhaps attempted them before, but unsuccessfully. Additionally, you must be careful not to disregard advice that, despite being well-known and useful, is occasionally disregarded or implemented improperly, putting the target at risk. Finally, reconditioning will enable you to develop fresh, resilient habits that will help you achieve wellness. So, until you achieve a certain level of spontaneity, you must repeat behaviors every day.

Returning To Good Health

You probably have been smoking for a while, and your fitness regimen is probably not up to par. Because smoking has an effect on the respiratory system, a smoker may find it difficult to breathe while performing even the simplest duties. After you begin to gradually cut back on smoking, which I hope this book has motivated you to do, you should think about increasing your exercise regimen. Exercise, as we all know, has many advantages and ought to be a top priority for everyone, but it is especially important for someone quitting smoking. In the beginning, it will assist strengthen your respiratory system, increase your energy, and give you a genuine sense of accomplishment.

Increase your everyday walking activities as your initial step, regardless of your degree of fitness. Get as much exercise as your body will comfortably allow, and as you build up strength and momentum, accelerate your pace to get your lungs functioning. Consider attending a reputable fitness center after you advance and feel more energized. Ideal amenities for this fitness center include a gym, a pool, a steam room, a sauna, and, if you really want to spoil yourself, a Jacuzzi. These hobbies are a terrific buddy to anyone quitting smoking since they each offer their own special advantages to help you enhance your health and well-being. These facilities have certified fitness instructors who can assist you in creating a weekly schedule that is specific to your requirements and skills. Perhaps a weightlifting regimen or some running might be more your style. I go to my neighborhood gym three times a week, and to avoid getting bored, I switch up my training routine every six to ten weeks. I regularly engage in weight training, swimming, jogging, cycling, stretching, and yoga classes. As a result, I currently feel better than I ever have. Even though I've passed my prime and am now in the second part of my life, I think my 25-year-old self would lose if we faced off in the ring.

You should start new, more advantageous activities to keep you busy as you quit smoking regularly. Avoid watching TV on the couch at home. You should avoid this area as much as possible because it is the only one where you will have intense impulses to smoke. It's vital to be active and engage in activities that will inspire you to continue on your new, better path. Be more extroverted and positive, and spend more time with your children or grandchildren. Become a member of a club or organization that will stimulate and entertain your thoughts. As you proceed, you'll be astonished by how much energy you start to have. Use it wisely on your favorite activities. A second chance in life, in your eyes.

You must be thinking how much harm all those cigarettes over the years have done to your heart, lungs, and throat, and whether or not it can be undone. Once more, I am not a medical professional, but based on my experience, I think that if the body is given the correct conditions to heal, it will start to undo the harm. Within weeks after quitting morning cigarettes, my cough began to subside. I started smoking at the age of nine, so my body wasn't even fully formed when I started smoking for at least 25 years. I haven't smoked in almost eight years now, and I feel better than ever. I recently completed a marathon, and even though I didn't win, I still finished in a respectable amount of time. My lungs and other organs were healthy and did not exhibit any symptoms of distress. That day, it was actually my legs that gave me the most trouble. For anyone worried about the potential health harm their smoking over the years may have caused them, that is a good testimonial.

The body's process of dying and regrowing cells is another way to look at its remarkable capacity for regeneration. For instance, I recently injured my finger while assisting a small elderly woman across the street; I'm kidding; I cut it carelessly while chopping a lemon in half. It began to bleed and sting. I washed it under the faucet, patted it dry, and applied a bandage. After a few days, I decided to leave it alone, and when I removed the bandage, it was healing as you might anticipate. I can't even tell which finger it was when I look at it now. Similar to how the rest of the body recovers and repairs itself, the National Library of Medicine claims that the heart may completely renew itself in three years. It follows that no portion of your heart from now existed more than three years ago. Your lungs go through the same procedure, although they renew much more quickly and are completely replaced in just one year. This tells me that you can expect your body to fully recover from years of smoking once you quit and give it the environment it needs to heal, such a healthy diet, exercise, and a stress-free lifestyle. This is excellent news that should soothe your concerns and put your mind at peace.

A family friend was diagnosed with throat and lung cancer a few years ago, and tragically, her prognosis was not good. He argued that there was no purpose in quitting smoking at this moment. Damage had already done. His family gathered and begged him to stop smoking because they believed it would prolong his life. He succeeded to quit as a result of adhering to their requests. He must have found it unbearable to hear such news and then decide to stop smoking, but he persisted. I guess it's amazing what grandkids' cries can do. He is still with us now and this was several years ago; he is still healthy. Therefore, I would say that it is never too late to stop smoking, regardless of the situation.

Selecting A Method For Quitting

• Prescription Drugs vs. Gradual vs. Cold Turkey Quitting

Cold turkey versus a gradual withdrawal

It is a noble decision to decide to stop smoking because doing so can have a positive impact on your health and quality of life. But one of the most important choices you'll have to make when starting this adventure is how to stop. Consideration is frequently given to two main strategies: abruptly ceasing to smoke or gradually cutting back. Each strategy has advantages and disadvantages, and ultimately, the one you choose will rely on your personal preferences, willpower, and lifestyle.

Go cold turkey:

When a smoker decides to quit abruptly, they do it without using nicotine replacement therapies (NRTs) or progressively cutting back. Consider the following when using this strategy:

Instantaneous Results: Cold turkey quitting has immediate results. You entirely give up smoking, immediately lowering your exposure to harmful substances.

No Prolonged Use of Nicotine: NRTs must be avoided while quitting cold turkey, according to some, who think this is the only way to break the cycle of addiction.

Strong effort Required: Since nicotine is not used in this technique, it necessitates a lot of effort to resist the physical and psychological impulses. For some people, this abrupt change may be challenging.

Higher Initial Discomfort Quitting smoking "cold turkey" can sometimes cause severe withdrawal symptoms in the first few days, including irritability, cravings, and mood swings. Possibility of mental and emotional weariness due to the nature of the activity.

Some People Benefit from Their Success: Some people believe that quitting smoking "cold turkey" is the most effective strategy since it results in a clean break from the habit as well as an immediate feeling of success.

The amount of smoking that a person does decreases over time, typically with the assistance of prescribed drugs or nicotine replacement therapies. When employing this tactic, take into consideration the following:

Reduced Withdrawal Symptoms: If you gradually cut back on your nicotine consumption, you may find that quitting becomes less of a challenge over time. It's possible that the withdrawal symptoms will be less severe and easier to handle.

Alternative treatments for nicotine dependence: NRTs, such as nicotine gum, patches, or lozenges, can help diminish a user's desire to smoke and give them a sense of control over the withdrawal symptoms they experience.

Psychological Preparation: If you quit smoking gradually, you'll give your mind time to get ready for the big quit by pinpointing the triggers that keep you smoking and developing strategies for dealing with them.

Because you wean yourself off of nicotine over the course of several weeks or months, this method may require more time on your part because of the slow tapering off process. It's possible that some people won't find it as inspiring or annoying as others do.

Risk of Relapse: If you quit smoking gradually, you run a greater risk of not being successful in achieving your goal. This is because some people are unable to persevere during prolonged reduction periods and will eventually start smoking again.

Choosing the Appropriate Approach Your preferences, resources, and the nature of the situation all factor into whether you should go suddenly or gradually. Take into consideration the following components:

The Dependence on Nicotine: If you have a serious nicotine addiction, quitting smoking "cold turkey" may be more difficult for you to do. A more gentle approach could consist of gradually weaning off of the use of NRTs.

Determining your level of resolution and determination to stop is an important aspect of willpower. If you have a strong determination and are prepared for an abrupt change, quitting cold turkey can be the best option for you.

Before deciding on a method, you should discuss it with a healthcare expert to ensure your health and safety. This is especially important if you have preexisting medical conditions. They will be able to provide you advice on what will ensure your safety the most.

Support System: Having a support system, such as friends, family, or a smoking cessation group, can be highly useful regardless of the route that you choose to take in order to quit smoking.

Adaptability: Take into account how you live your life and the routines you follow every day. It can be easier for you to take the stress of leaving gradually if you have a very busy schedule or are under a lot of pressure.

Find Yourself A Buddy With A Computer.

According to Bunny, one of the most important factors to consider in order to achieve success in discretion is to keep your focus on the goal you have set for yourself, despite the fact that doing so can be risky due to the fact that the potential benefits or drawbacks are not always immediately apparent.

Therefore, make the most of the days when you are not worrying about your long-term risk of cellular breakdown in the lungs or that retirement reserve by getting ahead of yourself. There are a number of websites, such as HealthyWage.com, DietBet.com, and GymPact, that provide monetary incentives for people to lose weight.

The goal defining step of stickK.com enables customers to create a "responsibility contract" on the target of their decision, which may include intellectual or relationship accomplishments as well as physical ones, such as getting in shape or improving their diet. StickK, which was developed by Yale College conduct business analysts, has racked up approximately 300,000 agreements and about $21 million in bets.

Customers have the ability to determine not only the stakes but also whether or whether unfortunate events are sent to family members, friends, or a charitable organization. In any event, Stick encourages its members to make the expense of their manner of behavior more expensive.

Hankering To Stop is a smoking cessation program that includes care as well as day-to-day registrations and an internet-based community to support clients in riding the flood of their wishes. For just one dollar per day, persons who need aid weaning off of cigarettes can check into Hankering To Stop. This smoking cessation program is available to people who need assistance weaning off of cigarettes.

The real care is also inherently rewarding. It is "an emergency signal" that smokers might have easily available in the situation in which they regularly smoke.There is a natural reward that comes with quitting smoking, and although distracting yourself from your cravings for cigarettes can be just what smokers need to overcome their addiction, there is no one method that is guaranteed to make it easier to exercise self-control.

There are a great number of approaches that can be interpreted across a variety of behaviors or addictions. "On the off chance that there was a one-size-fits-all, this sounds simple, truly,"

In point of fact, those who are attempting to change any manner of behavior should be prepared for accidents of some kind. Instead of giving up, you should try to learn from your mistake and consider how you might approach similar situations in the future with a different strategy.

Some smokers might think that the concept of quitting smoking "a little at a time" is straightforward and uncomplicated, but in actuality, this method can be challenging and even cruel to follow through with. This strategy, which is often referred to as the "reduction" technique, entails gradually cutting down on the amount of cigarettes smoked on a daily basis up until the point where the smoker is able to quit smoking altogether.

The difficulty with using this approach is that it is not an efficient technique to kick the habit of smoking. Cutting back on the amount of cigarettes smoked on a daily basis might cause withdrawal symptoms to last for a longer period of time, which can make quitting smoking an even more difficult task in the long term. Additionally, it demands a significant amount of support and encouragement from friends or family members, who will need to chat to the smoker on a daily basis and pretend to be encouraging, despite the fact that they dislike the smoker.

In addition, the strategy may be hard on the smoker's mental and physical well-being. Complaining is likely to begin when the smoker has reduced their daily cigarette consumption to 30 out of 40. The smoker will be in a state of moderate abstinence by the time they reach the third week, and by the time they reach the end of the first month, they will be in a state of significant cancellation. However, by the time they reach the 30th to the 39th day, they will have reached the most severe stage of withdrawal, during which they will be in excruciating pain and have nothing to show for their efforts.

One of the most significant drawbacks of this approach is the potential for it to result in relapse. The smoker will be in chronic abstinence after weeks or months of reducing the amount of cigarettes smoked, during which time they will be denying themselves 35–40 cigarettes on a daily basis; nonetheless, they will not be any closer to stopping smoking than the day they began the process. Furthermore, if the person who smokes is told that if things become tough, they may just take a hit every now and then to help them get through it, they will remain smoke-free for the rest of their lives.

In comparison, going cold turkey can be challenging but is not impossible to accomplish. The withdrawal symptoms will start to fade away after a period of three days. On the other hand, the severity of the withdrawal symptoms will continue to increase over the course of weeks, months, or even years if you cut back on the quantity of cigarettes you smoke.

In conclusion, giving up smoking is a journey that is unique to each individual, and it is essential to identify the way that is successful for them. The strategy of gradual detachment, often known as the "a little at a time" method, may not be the most effective method for quitting smoking because it can be stressful on both the mental and physical levels and can result in relapse. Instead, it is essential to have a conversation with your healthcare physician about the method that would work best for you and to formulate a strategy before you quit smoking. It is important to keep in mind that quitting smoking is a process that demands patience and determination, but the rewards for your health and well-being will make the effort more than worthwhile.

Maintaining healthy eating habits and enough water intake

Attaining and sustaining a healthy lifestyle, including quitting smoking, requires a number of critical lifestyle changes, including adopting healthy eating habits and ensuring adequate hydration. These behaviors can help you manage cravings and withdrawal symptoms, contribute to your overall well-being by providing needed nutrients, and provide essential support for your body. The following are some of the ways that maintaining a good diet and drinking enough water can help you quit smoking:

1. Consume a Diet That Is Well-Balanced: You should make it a priority to consume a diet that is well-balanced by consuming a mix of fruits, vegetables, whole grains, lean proteins, and healthy fats. A healthy, well-balanced diet contains the vital nutrients, vitamins, and minerals that are necessary for good

health, and it can assist in supporting your body's recovery from the harm caused by smoking.

2. Craving Management: Certain foods and beverages, such as those that are connected with smoking, might cause cravings or make them worse. Determine what sets off your own specific triggers and work on developing techniques to retrain your brain. If you typically smoked alongside your daily cup of coffee, for instance, you might want to think about switching to herbal tea or another beverage that is unrelated to smoking.

3. Pick Your Snacks Wisely: Make sure you always have access to nutritious food so that you can better control your desires and avoid mindless nibbling on harmful ones. Choose options that are high in nutrients, such as low-fat yogurt, fresh fruits and vegetables, nuts, and seeds. These snacks can offer a pleasing crunch, a natural sweetness, or a boost

in protein without contributing an excessive number of calories.

4. Maintain Adequate Hydration Keeping yourself adequately hydrated is vital for maintaining overall health and might assist in the management of cravings. Consume a lot of water throughout the day to maintain hydration and lessen the urge to engage in activities that require mouth stimulation. You can assist yourself remember to drink enough water every day by carrying a bottle of water with you wherever you go.

5. Maintain a Healthy Weight: Maintaining a healthy weight is a worry for some people during the process of quitting smoking. Choose your foods with awareness, pay attention to maintaining proper portion control, and recognize the role that your emotions play in how much you eat. As was said previously, including regular physical activity in one's routine can also help

one achieve their weight management goals.

6. Practice mindful eating by paying attention to the tastes, sensations, and textures of the food you eat when you are engaging in this practice of mindful eating. Take your time and really relish each bite to get the most out of the meal and the experience of eating. consuming with awareness not only fosters a more positive relationship with food but also helps prevent consuming too much of it.

7. Stay away from excessive amounts of caffeine and alcohol: Both caffeine and alcohol have been linked to increased cigarette cravings and could sabotage your efforts to quit smoking. Reduce the amount of caffeinated beverages, such as coffee, tea, and energy drinks, that you drink each day. Be careful about how much alcohol you drink because drinking might weaken your inhibitions and make it more likely that you will relapse.

8. Consume an Adequate Amount of Fiber: Adding foods that are high in fiber to your diet, such as whole grains, legumes, fruits, and vegetables, will assist support digestion, promote satiety, and help prevent constipation, which can be a common concern during smoking cessation.

Keep in mind that changing your eating habits will require effort and patience on your part. Instead of striving for perfection, concentrate on making progress. Be kind to yourself if you mess up occasionally while you're making the transition to eating healthier options at each meal and snack and do it gradually. The goal is to develop a way of life that is not only healthy but also environmentally friendly and beneficial to one's entire health.

If you have specific dietary problems or questions, it is best to contact with a registered dietitian or other healthcare expert who can provide individualized recommendations based on your individual needs and health goals. If you have specific dietary concerns or questions, it is best to talk with a trained dietitian or another healthcare practitioner.

As a final piece of advice, don't forget to enjoy your victories along the road and reward yourself with non-food-related treats or activities as a kind of positive reinforcement for your commitment to living a healthier and smoke-free life. Celebrating your successes is a great way to stay motivated and on track with your goals.

Maintaining Your Resilience It takes resilience and commitment to manage the cravings and withdrawal symptoms that come with stopping use of an addictive substance. Remind yourself that these sensations will pass and are a natural part of the process of getting better. You are demonstrating to yourself that you are strong and strengthening your dedication to the diet with each craving that you are able to overcome.

Gaining Wisdom via Adversity

It is essential to keep in mind that dealing with obstacles does not equate to being a failure. You will gain invaluable experience and a deeper understanding of your triggers and coping techniques for cravings and withdrawal symptoms as you persevere through each challenge and emerge victorious.

Acceptance of the Procedure:

Getting a handle on your cravings and the symptoms of withdrawal is an essential aspect of beating your smoking habit. You are laying the groundwork for long-term success by confronting these problems with a combination of strategies, a supportive network, and a resolve to succeed. This will set the stage for long-term success. Every action you take is a demonstration of your commitment to living a life that is free from the harmful effects of smoking.

Restoring Your Health by Caring for Your Body

Not only does giving up cigarettes allow you to break free of the grip of nicotine addiction, but it also presents a significant chance to restore your body's health and wellness. Your decision to stop smoking is a statement of self-care and empowerment in its own right. You are laying the groundwork for a life that is full of vitality and does not involve smoking when you cultivate healthy habits, nurture your body, and embrace well-being.

Putting an Emphasis on Nutrition:

Diet That Is Balanced: A diet that is rich in fruits, vegetables, lean meats, whole grains, and healthy fats should be the primary focus of your eating habits. These nutrients aid in the body's natural process of healing and supply it with the vital energy it needs.

Water intake: Consuming a lot of water will help wash toxins out of your system and keep your body's functions running smoothly. Other beverages that can help you stay hydrated include herbal teas and natural juices. Limit Processed meals: Try to limit your intake of processed meals that are high in sugar, salt, and harmful fats. Choose foods that are entire, high in nutrients, and provide fuel for your body.

Activities Involving Movement:

Maintaining a Regular Exercise Routine
It is recommended that you maintain a regular exercise routine in order to improve your cardiovascular health, raise your mood, and better handle stress. Find things that you take pleasure in doing so that you may turn exercise into a habit that will stick with you.

Aerobic and Strength Training: To attain a well-rounded fitness regimen, include a combination of aerobic exercises (such as walking, swimming, or cycling) and strength training (with weights or resistance bands). Examples of aerobic workouts include walking, swimming, or cycling.

Sleep and the Management of Stress

Consider the following: Doze off: Aim to get between 7 and 9 hours of restful sleep every night. Develop a soothing pattern for winding down before bed, ensure that your sleeping environment is always pleasant, and have a regular sleep schedule.

Reducing Stress: To reduce stress, engage in activities such as meditation, deep breathing, yoga, or hobbies, or practice stress-reduction strategies such as these. Stress management can help prevent relapses and is beneficial to your general health and well-being.

Pay close attention to your dental hygiene as part of your commitment to respecting your body. Your oral health can be improved by practicing good dental hygiene on a consistent basis. This includes brushing, flossing, and going to the dentist regularly.

Quitting smoking is one of the best things you can do for your skin because it can enhance both its appearance and its texture. Create a skincare routine to provide your skin with the nutrients it needs to combat the negative effects of smoking and speed up its recovery.

Self-care through mindfulness:

Practices That Help You Relax: Participate in activities that are known to promote relaxation, such as taking hot baths, getting massages, or spending time in nature. These hobbies are great for relaxing and helping you wind down at the end of the day.

Meditation and Mindfulness: Putting these two practices into practice can help you be more present in the moment and develop a more optimistic outlook. Stress reduction and an overall improvement in mental health are two benefits that might accrue from regular meditation practice.

Regarding Your Ongoing Support

As I mentioned in chapter 2, this book is a self-help guide that is suitable for light smokers who smoke ten cigarettes per day, moderate smokers who smoke twenty cigarettes per day, and heavy smokers who smoke more than fifty cigarettes per day. In addition to the strategy, you will need someone to hold your hand and provide you with ongoing support if you are a heavy smoker who smokes more than 20 cigarettes per day or a chain smoker. You can reach me through my email address, which is 79.siva.gd@gmail.com. I am a Master NLP Practitioner, a Master hypnotherapist, a coach, and a trainer. I can guide you with additional techniques that could be of considerable help in quitting smoking. If you are interested in working with me, please contact me.

You can reach out to me at the e-mail address listed above if you have any questions about how to execute the approach, if you believe that you require hand-holding or any other form of ongoing assistance on your road to quit smoking, or if you run into any doubts while implementing the technique.

What if I failed at some point along the way? What if I went backwards either while I was on the journey or after I had successfully finished it? You can contact me by any of these channels, including my email address.

This book will come to a close with a brief explanation of the concept of habit.

The definition of the word "habit" is "something that you do frequently and almost without thinking," with the emphasis being on "something that is difficult to stop doing."

So when you first started smoking, you would have given it some thought, but in the long term, if it has become a habit, the amount of time spent thinking about it is significantly reduced to a millisecond, or sometimes you don't even think about it at all. You never have any reason to smoke other than the fact that you do. Therefore, while you aren't thinking, the mind isn't playing its usual part in the situation. As a result, the primary focus of this method is on conditioning your body to tolerate the more than 7,000 chemicals that are found in cigarettes.

MANY GRATITUDES

Warnings and caveats:

1. Some background on the method: I first learned about this method in the year 2006; it was written down and posted in a medical facility, but I can't even recall the name of the hospital where I saw it. Due to the fact that there are six doctors practicing medicine in my extended family, I used to go to a lot

of hospitals. As a result, I couldn't remember which hospital it was.

Whether or not this method has been validated by scientific research is not something I can comment on.

Simply said, I discovered this method more than 16 years ago in 2006, put it into practice on myself, and was finally able to kick my smoking habit for good. When it is functioning well for me, it ought to also function well for any average individual who is similar to me. As a result, I decided to write a book in order to impart this information to other people.

2. With regard to the aforementioned Physical Activities: You should only participate in any of the aforementioned physical activities if you are physically able and fit to do so. Please see a physiotherapist if you are having any problems; they will be happy to assist you.

3. The effectiveness of the self-talk that was discussed in Chapter 9 increases with the number of times you repeat it to yourself while increasing the volume of your delivery.

Why Do You Even Bother To Start Smoking In The First Place?

Because we as humans have such a strong desire for pleasure and contentment, we are susceptible to being swayed by the glitter that lies just below the surface.

We neglect the genuine meaning of happiness and contentment in favor of addiction—to food, lifestyle, cellphones, and in your case, smoking. We do this because we believe that addiction will bring us happiness and satisfaction.

You see, when you engage in an activity that brings you pleasure, your brain sends a signal that makes you wish for more of that sensation.

This is the reason why our love for cookies, sex, food, a dress, smoking, and drink rarely. infrequently. The subsequent result is the development of an addiction, the recovery from which calls for hard work and perseverance.

The urges keep flowing, like a surge of adrenaline, and they force you to tap into a different and more unconscious side of yourself that you had no idea existed in order to meet your wants.

Dopamine, a neurotransmitter that is released by the brain and is responsible for making you feel good, is the reason why you have that feeling of wanting more. Addiction is a direct result of excessive dopamine.

Dopamine is essential to living a healthy and normal life. It affects everything from learning and attention to movement, emotion, and sleep, as well as blood vessel and kidney function, lactation, heart rate, pain processes, and, of course, concentration. It also controls the rate at which the heart beats.

The important takeaway from this is that there is no question that an adequate supply of dopamine is beneficial to both the body and the brain. Dopamine, on the other hand, is able to comprehend pleasure, and it causes an intense desire to relive the moment repeatedly. If, on the other hand, you resist giving in to your desires, the dopamine in your brain will go looking for gratification in other parts of your body.

Dopamine is responsible for transmitting impulses throughout the body, ultimately arriving at their destination in the brain. It is the source of the sensations of pleasure, motivation, and fulfillment that you experience as a direct result of the things that you accomplish, appreciate, and perceive.

A dopamine level that is low is not a desirable state to be in. It diminishes your ability to sense pleasure and makes you feel less motivated, hesitant, tired, restless, and melancholy. It also helps you feel less tired.

It is also possible to generate an excessively high level of dopamine in a specific portion of your body in comparison to other parts, which can lead to addiction, violence, binge eating, impulsive buying, and an extremely competitive personality.

When you smoke, the high level of nicotine in the cigarette raises your dopamine level, which in turn makes you crave more nicotine to put into your body. You might be wondering, "What is nicotine?"

Nicotine is the primary factor contributing to the difficulty of quitting smoking. It is a substance that causes addiction and can be found in tobacco products, cigarettes, and vaporizers. It is possible to get dependent on it due to the fact that, after being absorbed into the bloodstream, it transmits messages to the brain and triggers the release of dopamine. Keep in mind that you teach the brain what it remembers by what you give it to eat. Let's speak about some of the reasons why you could have started smoking in the first place:

Pressure from Peers

It's possible that you smoke due to the influence of other people. It has been a significant factor in the narratives that people tell about why they participate in any activity, but particularly vices. A subtle and pressing sense that makes you want to fit in can arise from having friends of different or comparable ages. This pressure could come from having pals.

Keep in mind that it's quite fine if you don't fit in, and in fact, it's much better when you appreciate who you really are.

Reduction of stress and fury, as well as pain, and promotion of tranquility

No matter how fleeting the effect may be, it is a well-known fact that smoking can help relieve stress as well as unwelcoming moods and ignite tranquility within you. The pressures of modern life are sufficient to cause anyone to feel the need to seek relief in the form of smoking. It's also likely that smoking helps you get over your fears of public speaking, including nervousness and shyness.

A surge of motivation as well as an increase in hormones

Many people start smoking because they need the boost of energy it provides in order to engage in certain activities, whether those activities are pleasurable or not. In actuality, the source of motivation is found within a person; nonetheless, individuals continue to believe that it derives from outside influences. It's possible that you are a believer as well, and that's perfectly OK.

A surge of creative energy

This happens frequently in the entertainment and creative industries on all levels. Because you believe that under its influence you are better able to focus, you may smoke in the hopes of triggering your creative mode and coming up with something truly exceptional. You could be right; many present and former smokers can witness to this fact; nevertheless, there is a more effective alternative.

Because of its importance to education

Young adults and teenagers, most commonly students in high school, frequently smoke cigarettes in order to improve their concentration in class and during other school-related activities. Typically, it's in order to fulfill the performance requirements for tests, lessons, and various other activities.

Believe it or not, whatever reason or reasons strike a chord with you, I get it. I can empathize with your intense desire to breeze over challenges and indulge in pleasurable experiences as soon as humanly possible. If you keep reading, I'll explain the reasons why you should quit smoking as well as the steps you need to do to do so.

Taking Charge of Your Life Without Tobacco

Congratulations on achieving your goal of quitting smoking and becoming a healthier non-smoker! Throughout the course of this book, we have discussed the various stages of quitting smoking, as well as the drawbacks of traditional methods and the potent strategies generated from effective methods such as Allen Carr's Easy Way to Stop Smoking. We have gone through the significance of developing a solid support network, gaining an awareness of nicotine withdrawal symptoms, avoiding falling back into old habits, and maintaining long-term success. It's time to celebrate your success in quitting smoking and enjoy the smoke-free life you've created for yourself.

You have wonderful strength, drive, and resilience for having made it this far despite the difficulty of giving up smoking. You have the ability to break free from the chains of nicotine addiction and create a future that is full of health, energy, and independence if you follow the tactics that are explained in this book and use the resources that you have gained.

As you go into this next phase of your life, it is essential that you keep a few things in mind, including the following:

1. Consider the path you've traveled: Take some time now to think about the journey you've been on and the strides you've made forward. Recognize the difficulties you've defeated, the hurdles you've gotten beyond, and the growth you've experienced over the course of your life. You should be proud of the resilience and perseverance you've displayed throughout this process. Keep in mind that kicking the habit of smoking is a major accomplishment, and you have every right to feel proud of yourself for accomplishing this goal.

2. Take advantage of the improvements to your health that will occur as a result of quitting smoking: this is one of the most significant advantages of kicking the habit. Consider the many ways in which your body has improved since you quit smoking and give yourself some credit for it. Your cardiovascular system

is getting stronger, your lungs are getting healthier, and the danger of you contracting a variety of ailments is going down. Recognize and appreciate the fact that you have made a major progress in living a life that is both healthier and longer.

3. Make the most of the financial advantages Quitting smoking is not only good for your health but also delivers money advantages. Think about how much cash you've been able to save ever since you kicked the habit of smoking. Consider the ways in which you can put this more cash to use to improve other aspects of your life, such as following your interests, going on the vacation of your dreams, or advancing your own professional and personal growth. Take full advantage of the increased financial independence that comes with quitting smoking.

4. Embrace your newfound freedom: Once you quit smoking, you are no longer constrained by the requirement to smoke cigarettes. Embrace the freedom that comes with being emancipated from the cravings, the social stigma, and the dependency on nicotine. This freedom is yours to enjoy once you have successfully kicked the habit. Take pleasure in the fact that you can participate fully in activities without having to interrupt them for smoke breaks. Embrace the freedom to breathe clean air, smell the scents of the world around you, and live life to the fullest by giving up smoking so that you can do so.

5. Develop practices of self-care: Now that you are a non-smoker, making self-care a top priority is extremely important. Participate in pursuits that provide mental, physical, and spiritual sustenance to you. Maintaining a healthy

body and a vibrant state of mind requires consistent movement in the form of exercise. Investigate various methods of relaxation such as yoga, meditation, or deep breathing in order to lower your stress level and improve your general health. Maintaining a healthy emotional state can be accomplished through cultivating positive connections, partaking in activities and interests that bring you joy, and making time for introspection and personal development.

6. Tell others about your experience and motivate them: The process you went through to quit smoking was not only meaningful for you, but it also has the potential to inspire other people. Give others who are having trouble quitting smoking the benefit of your experience, your strength, and your hope. Someone who is looking for a means to break their

addiction to nicotine could find inspiration and encouragement in your tale. You give other people the confidence to take charge of their own health and make great changes in their lives when you share your experience with them.

7. Don't let your guard down and don't give up Although you have come a long way on your road to quit smoking, it is crucial that you keep your wits about you and don't give up. The dependency on nicotine is a tremendous force, and during recovery, you may have periods of temptation or triggers. Maintain your resolve to quit smoking completely and completely. Make efficient use of the methods and strategies you've learned to get through hard situations and satisfy urges in a healthy way. Always keep in mind that you are more

powerful than any momentary want to smoke a cigarette.

8. Open yourself up to the possibilities: Because you don't smoke, you've given yourself access to a whole new realm of opportunities. Put this newly found freedom and energy to good use by going after your aspirations, setting lofty objectives for yourself, and trying out new things. Make the most of your chance to reimagine who you are and live a life that is full with joy, purpose, and passion. Accept the opportunities that lie in wait for you and approach each day with an attitude of thankfulness and excitement.

The Dangers Of Smoking To One's Health

The unhealthy habit of smoking has a major negative effect on a person's overall health and should be avoided at all costs. In this chapter, we will discuss the numerous health hazards that are linked with smoking, including the impact that smoking has on the body both immediately and over a longer period of time. Those who smoke can find the motivation to quit smoking and improve their health and well-being just by learning about the negative effects smoking has on the body.

Quitting smoking has a number of positive effects on one's health and can have a significant positive impact on one's quality of life. However, chronic smokers stand to benefit from having a better understanding of the dangers that are inherent in their habit, which are discussed in the following paragraphs.

Immediate threats to one's health posed by smoking include a slower heart rate, higher blood pressure, and a decrease in the amount of oxygen that can reach the heart and other organs. These consequences can lead to an increased chance of having a heart attack or a stroke, in addition to other cardiovascular disorders.

The negative effects of smoking on one's health over the long term are considerably more serious and include a wide variety of life-threatening illnesses, such as the following:

1 Cardiovascular diseases The chance of having a heart attack, stroke, and other cardiovascular diseases is increased

when a person smokes. Tobacco smoke contains chemicals that can cause damage to the heart and blood arteries, which can lead to a buildup of plaque. This plaque buildup can create blood clots, which can result in a heart attack or a stroke.

2 Cancer: Smoking is the leading preventable cause of mortality from cancer, making it the second leading cause of death overall. It raises the chance of numerous different types of cancer, including cancer of the lung, throat, and mouth as well as cancer of the bladder, pancreas, and kidneys.

3 disorders with the respiratory system Smoking can lead to a variety of respiratory disorders, the most common of which are chronic obstructive pulmonary disease (COPD), emphysema, bronchitis, and pneumonia. The airways can become damaged from smoking, which can make it difficult to breathe

and can also raise the chance of developing lung infections.

4. Decreased fertility Smoking can have an effect on male and female fertility, lowering the chances of successfully conceiving a child and raising the likelihood of experiencing a miscarriage or giving birth prematurely.

Smokers have a much lower life expectancy than non-smokers do as a result of their habit, which is the fifth reason why smoking is bad for you. Smokers have a mortality rate that is on average ten years earlier than non-smokers.

Reduced physical fitness Smoking can lower a person's physical fitness and limit their capacity to participate in physical exercise, both of which can contribute to a decline in their overall health and well-being.

7 Problems with the teeth and gums Smoking can cause discoloration of the teeth, gum disease, and even the loss of teeth.

8 Skin issues Smoking is known to hasten the aging process of the skin, which can result in wrinkles and discolouration.

9 A diminished sense of smell and taste Smoking can impair a person's sense of smell and taste, making it more difficult for them to appreciate the flavors of food and other sensory experiences.

To summarize, smoking is a harmful habit that is associated with a multitude of health hazards, both in the short term and the long term. Quitting smoking is one of the finest things a person can do for their health and well-being. Smokers can quit smoking and enjoy the many benefits of a smoke-free life provided they have access to the appropriate tools and resources. Quitting smoking is one of the best things a person can do for their health and well-being.

Putting The Pieces In Place For Victory

Getting ready to quit smoking requires mental and emotional preparation on your part. Developing a positive and encouraging atmosphere.

In this section, we will discuss how to get yourself mentally and emotionally ready to give up smoking.

1.1 Contemplating Your Driving Forces and Desires

It is critical that you take some time to think about why you want to stop smoking before you start the process of quitting smoking. Could you take some time to think about and document the reasons you wish to leave this job? Clarifying your reasons for wanting to quit smoking may serve as a powerful reminder and a source of determination while you work through the process of quitting smoking. These reasons may include improving your health, setting a good example for loved ones, or regaining control over your life.

1.2 Establishing Goals That Are Compatible with Reality

Quitting smoking is a huge undertaking, and it is crucial that you set reasonable goals for yourself in this process. Take into account the fact that leaving may not be simple, but it is still doable. Acknowledge the possibility that you will face obstacles on the journey, but take comfort in the knowledge that you are able to triumph over such obstacles because to your perseverance and strength. You will be able to approach the process of quitting with a balanced perspective and decrease the unneeded strain you are putting on yourself if you set realistic expectations for yourself.

1.3 The Practice of Fostering an Optimistic Attitude

A positive mental attitude is one of the most important factors in effectively stopping smoking. Change your viewpoint to look at the positive sides of leaving instead of concentrating on the challenges or sacrifices that you believe will be required. Seize the chance to make positive changes to your health, reclaim your power, and build a smoke-free future for yourself. You can create and keep a positive mindset throughout your journey by practicing positive self-affirmations, using techniques that involve visualization, and surrounding yourself with positive influences.

Developing a Conducive Setting is Covered in Section 2 of This Guide.

2.1 Seek Out the Companionship of Your Loved Ones

Having a strong support system makes quitting smoking much more manageable for most people. Get in touch with your loved ones, as well as your friends and family, and let them know that you have decided to move on. You should ask them for their support, encouragement, and understanding. During difficult circumstances, having a network of individuals who believe in you and the objective you're working toward can provide both emotional support and accountability.

2.2 Participate in Community Organizations

Could you join support groups or online communities that are solely devoted to helping people give up smoking, in addition to receiving encouragement from the people in your immediate circle? These communities offer a protected environment in which members may talk about their experiences, seek the guidance of those who are going through something similar, and receive inspiration from those around them. Participating in activities with people who share your interests can provide you with priceless support, sources of inspiration, and useful pointers that can help you maintain your motivation and dedication.

2.3 Make Adjustments to Your Physical Surroundings

Changing your physical surroundings so that there are fewer triggers and temptations is one way to create a supportive atmosphere for yourself. Take all smoking materials, including cigarettes, lighters, and ashtrays, out of your home, vehicle, and place of business. Remove the odor and any visual cues that remind you of smoking by thoroughly cleaning and sanitizing the associated locations. To strengthen your resolve to kick the habit of smoking, you might want to think about making your home a smoke-free zone. By making adjustments to your surrounding environment, you can get rid of potential roadblocks and make a location that is conducive to your smoke-free existence.

In conclusion, getting oneself psychologically and emotionally ready for the challenge of quitting smoking and surrounding yourself with positive influences are essential components of a winning strategy. Your resolution and determination can be strengthened by taking some time to think about what drives you, by establishing goals for yourself that are attainable, and by maintaining a positive mental attitude. You can reduce the likelihood of experiencing triggers by seeking assistance from loved ones, being involved in communities that are accepting, and making adjustments to your physical environment. By intentionally taking steps to improve your chances of quitting smoking, you can raise the likelihood that you will be successful. The next chapters will provide you with additional support on your quest to stop smoking by delving into useful tactics, natural aids, and helpful hints along the way.

The reduction in air pollution, waste, and the consumption of natural resources that results from giving up smoking is another way that quitting smoking helps the environment.

Reduced levels of air pollution: Cigarette smoke is known to contain thousands of harmful compounds, all of which are known to contribute to air pollution. Quitting smoking is the single most important thing you can do to improve the health of those around you as well as the overall quality of the air we breathe.

Reduced waste: cigarette butts are one of the most common forms of litter. They don't decompose for many years and release harmful chemicals into the environment. Quitting smoking is one of the best things you can do for the environment because it cuts down on trash and the damage it does to ecosystems.

In order to produce tobacco and cigarettes, large amounts of water, energy, and land are required. This highlights the importance of preserving these natural resources. Quitting smoking is an important step toward a more sustainable future as it helps to conserve these resources and reduces one's carbon footprint.

Enhanced General Quality of Life

Quitting smoking can result in an overall improvement in your quality of life, as you will experience better health, increased energy, and a more optimistic outlook:

Quitting smoking can lead to improved circulation and increased oxygen levels in the blood, both of which can result in increased energy levels and improved physical performance.

Improved quality of sleep Smoking can cause insomnia and disrupt normal sleep patterns. Giving up smoking can lead to an improvement in sleep quality, which in turn can leave you feeling more rested and revitalized.

Reduced levels of stress and anxiety: Despite the fact that studies has shown that smoking actually raises levels of tension and anxiety, many people who smoke are under the impression that cigarettes help to reduce stress. Putting an end to one's smoking habit might lead to greater stress management as well as mental wellness.

In conclusion, the advantages of giving up smoking are numerous and widespread, having an effect on almost every facet of your life. The benefits of giving up smoking are truly life-changing, ranging from enhancements to one's health and financial situation to enhancements to one's relationships as well as to the environment. Keep these benefits in mind as you continue on your journey, and allow them to serve as incentive for you to keep your commitment to leading a life that is healthier and happier.

Although nicotine can improve your mental function, it also has the effect of diminishing your sense of self-worth over time. When you make the decision to cease, your conviction is called into question.

You are frequently persuaded by other people by listening to them share their own experiences, which results in a relapse after you have quit smoking. Perhaps we might take some solace in the fact that, in response to our instructions, they have started smoking cigarettes with larger filters.

an incompetent expert because, for some reason, people have the misconception that larger filtered cigarettes are safer. We are of the opinion that continuing to smoke cigarettes, regardless of the number of cigarettes smoked or the size of their filters, indicates that one is still dependent on tobacco.

There are many different therapy options available for people who want to quit smoking. One of the healthiest and most all-natural approaches to treatment is the acupuncture method. Because of the way that smoking affects your taste buds, you might find that you wish to give up the habit. As soon as you take that first drag after beginning acupuncture treatment, the flavor will start to deteriorate. In most cases, we will recommend that you go to a therapist or see a doctor in order to make your life simpler; but, we will insist that you choose the more challenging option by being willing to make the necessary sacrifices. If you are able to achieve success just a few days after considering quitting up, we guarantee that your level of self-assurance will never decrease again. I was able to kick the habit without the use of any medications or therapies. You can show yourself that you are in charge of both your environment and your enthusiasm by doing something to indicate this. Due to the fact that this is advise that is so general, it will be different from person to person depending on their mental capacity. In addition, we strongly recommend that you conduct a self-examination in order to establish whether or not you require the assistance of an outside therapist. You should do this without ignoring the counsel of your own inner voice. Even conventional medical institutions such as Holistic Healthcare Online offer alternative medicine therapies for the withdrawal symptoms that come after quitting smoking. It's possible that hypnosis and Penn therapy could be helpful in minimizing the negative effects of quitting smoking.

As a direct consequence of this, the difficulty will grow. People who have minds that aren't very strong might start to think that they aren't useful anymore and that everything around them is worthless and boring even. These people might feel let down given the circumstances of their lives. As a result, making the decision to quit smoking is a form of punishment. Anyone can inquire, "Then why do you continue to do it? Another impression that takes you back in time right away is the one that goes, "Instead, let me not become the butt of laughs and start swimming with the flow again." What possible harm might come from smoking just one cigarette? is yet another idea that might occur to you at this very moment. Bear in mind, however, that making a decision is a much more challenging task than attempting to explain that decision later on.

As a result, why go back after having already finished the most essential stage of staying with an audacious decision when you could just keep going? Despite the fact that one has been spared a lot, the long-term consequences of nicotine may cause one's energy level to decrease to a certain extent.

disease that is very close to being fatal Have you ever given any regard to the notion that the dizziness you feel will only last for a short while? Why don't you try to convince yourself that you have been successful in overcoming the dreaded nicotine when the majority of people fail to do so? You appear to be operating on a mental level that is distinct from others, don't you? Think and behave in a constructive manner.

One way to adopt a more positive view is to perform a calculation to determine the financial advantage. First things first, calculate how much money you have put away so far today. What does the balance of $2 look like after it has been there for five days?

As a result, you are making significant financial preparations for your household, your offspring, or, at the absolute least, for your way of life. At least you are not throwing away money; rather, you are utilizing it to entertain yourself. Tell yourself that you can do it, and then go ahead and do it! In 365 days, we'll go on yet another wonderful excursion! In all seriousness, $770!

The Easiest Way To End Your Addiction To Cigarettes

Putting an end to one's smoking habit is not always an easy task. Having said that, it is possible if you are well-prepared. Consider the following steps that Josh followed in order to kick his smoking habit:

The majority of people who use tobacco experience intense desires to smoke or crave tobacco on a regular basis. Despite this, you have the ability to control your urges.

Keep in mind that the temptation to use tobacco, even if it is intense, will probably disappear within five to ten minutes, regardless of whether you light a cigarette or take a dip of chewing tobacco. This is true whether you smoke a cigarette or take a dip of chewing tobacco. Every time you successfully fight off a craving for tobacco, you move closer to beating your addiction once and for all.

When the need to smoke or use tobacco products arises, the following 10 tactics can assist you in avoiding giving in to it.

1. Give replacement therapy for nicotine some thought.

Talk to your primary care provider about starting a nicotine replacement therapy program. Among the available options are:

Nicotine can be administered via inhaler or as a nasal splash.

Nicotine patches, gum, and capsules are available for purchase without the need for a prescription.

A way out drugs that do not include nicotine for quitting smoking, such as bupropion and varenicline

You may find that short-acting nicotine replacement therapies, such as nicotine gum, pills, nasal sprays, or inhalers, are helpful for overcoming intense cravings. These short-acting therapies are generally safe to use, and they can be used in conjunction with long-acting nicotine patches or one of the medications that do not contain nicotine for the purpose of quitting smoking.

Recently, there has been a lot of interest in using electronic cigarettes (also known as e-cigarettes) as an alternative to smoking traditional cigarettes. However, there is no evidence to suggest that electronic cigarettes are either safer or more effective in the treatment of smoking cessation than drugs that contain nicotine replacement therapy.

2. Stay away from any potential triggers

It's likely that the places where you smoke or chew tobacco the most, like parties or bars, as well as stressful situations or while you're drinking coffee, will trigger the highest cravings in you to smoke or chew tobacco. Develop a plan to navigate around or steer clear of your triggers so you can quit smoking without resorting to tobacco.

Make every effort to avoid putting yourself in a position where you will experience a smoking backslide. If you frequently smoke while talking on the phone, for example, keep a pen and paper nearby so that you may draw instead of smoking. This will help you kick the habit.

3. If you feel the want to give in to your craving for cigarettes, tell yourself that in order to do so, you must first wait an additional 10 minutes.

After that, fill that time with anything productive to keep you from getting bored. Try going to a public place without lighting up any tobacco products. With the help of these simple strategies, you might be able to conquer the desire to smoke tobacco.

4. If you chew on it, it will offer your mouth something to do, which will help you avoid the want to smoke tobacco.

Chew some gum that doesn't contain sugar, or some hard candies. An other option for a snack that is both crunchy and tasty is to munch on raw carrots, almonds, or sunflower seeds.

5. Never have "just one" cigarette. If you have an intense need for cigarettes, you can find yourself tempted to smoke just one.

You should not, however, trick yourself into believing that you have reached the end of the process. Having only one typically leads to having more than one. In addition to this, there is a possibility that you will start using cigarettes again.

6. Keeping your body active can assist you in forgetting about the want to smoke cigarettes.

Even short spurts of movement, like as sprinting up and down the stairs multiple times, might satisfy a craving for cigarettes. This is because the nicotine in tobacco stimulates the body's release of endorphins. Take a stroll or a jog around the neighborhood.

You can get a good workout at home or at work by performing exercises such as squats, deep knee bends, pushups, sprinting in place, or going up and down a set of stairs. If you are able to get by without doing any active job, you might want to try praying, doing some sewing or woodworking, or keeping a journal. On the other side, you could accomplish the chores that were interrupted, such as cleaning or documenting the paperwork.

7. If you smoked as a means of relieving stress, you should give relaxation techniques a try instead.

The struggle to resist a want to smoke tobacco can be stressful in and of itself. In order to relax and alleviate tension, you can try deep breathing, muscular relaxation, yoga, visualization, massage, or listening to music that is comforting.

8. If you are having trouble fighting the need to smoke, talk to someone who can help you, such as a friend, family member, or member of a support group.

You may talk to each other over the phone, go on a stroll, have a little bit of fun, or meet together so that you can talk to each other and support each other. Counseling is another option that may be helpful.

9. For more help on your journey to quit smoking, enroll in an online program.

You might also read a blog written by someone who has successfully kicked the habit of smoking and offer support to people who are also fighting the urge to smoke. Discover how other people have conquered their urges to smoke by studying their experiences.

10. Jot down or verbalize the reasons why you wish to quit smoking and resist the urges to smoke tobacco products.

Remind yourself of the benefits that come with it. Some of these reasons could be: the desire to save money, the want to feel better, or the desire to improve one's health. Keep in mind that it is always preferable to make an effort to quit using cigarettes rather than doing nothing at all to achieve this goal. In addition, every time you fight the need to have a cigarette, you get a little bit closer to a life in which you don't use tobacco.

Becoming A Member Of Support Groups As Well As Online Communities

You don't have to go through the difficulties of quitting smoking by yourself if that's something you want to do. Participating in quitting smoking support groups in person or participating in online forums can be a real game-changer for someone who is trying to kick the habit. These communities offer a secure and encouraging environment in which members may meet others who share their interests, discuss their pasts, learn from one another's observations, and find the inspiration they require to keep pushing forward with their goals. In the following paragraphs, we will discuss the advantages of participating in support groups and online communities, as well as the ways in which doing so can considerably increase the likelihood that you will be able to quit smoking successfully.

1. Comprehending and Empathy: Support groups and online communities are made up of people who are either presently undergoing the process of quitting smoking themselves or who have previously been successful in doing so. They have an understanding of the difficulties, urges, and emotional upheaval that come along with giving up smoking. By becoming a member of one of these communities, you put yourself in a position to be understood by others who share similar life experiences to your own. It may be really reassuring and validating to talk about your struggles and successes with others who fully comprehend what you are going

through and share your views and experiences with them.

2. A Platform for the Exchange of Experiences and Insights: Support groups and online communities provide a venue for the exchange of personal experiences and observations. You can get knowledge from those who have already conquered the challenge of quitting smoking by participating in group meetings, forums, and debates. You will have the opportunity to obtain useful knowledge about useful tactics, coping processes, and ideas for managing cravings. Hearing about other people's triumphs and gaining knowledge from those who have successfully kicked the habit of smoking can serve as a source of inspiration and motivation for your own path. The collective knowledge and first-hand experiences that are shared within these

networks can provide members with new insights and novel strategies for kicking their smoking habit.

3. A Non-Judgmental atmosphere One of the most significant benefits of support groups and online communities is the atmosphere in which they provide, which is one that does not pass judgment on its members. You are able to freely communicate your opinions, worries, and issues in these settings without the risk of being judged or stigmatized for doing so. Because of the widespread acceptance and understanding that permeates these communities, members feel a sense of security that enables them to be open and honest about the challenges they face. This welcoming environment not only encourages open discussion but also helps lessen emotions of isolation

and humiliation, both of which can be associated with quitting smoking.

People Who Try To Quit Smoking May Find It Simpler To Do So If They Follow These Suggestions.

For smokers who are attempting to kick the habit, quitting smoking can be a process that is not only exceedingly difficult but also extremely irritating. Quitting smoking can be a very difficult and challenging chore because nicotine is such an effective and potent substance of addiction. The task can be exceedingly difficult and challenging. Because there are so many resources on the internet geared at assisting people who are trying to kick the habit of smoking, it is currently much less difficult to make the decision to stop smoking for good and to follow through with the actions that are required to do so. In point of fact, it is simpler than it has ever been. Here are five useful suggestions that will help you kick the habit of smoking for good!

If you are ready to, giving up smoking is the best decision you can make for your health and should be your top priority. Smoking cigarettes is associated with a wide variety of detrimental impacts on a person's physical health. However, it is not always evident which strategy of quitting smoking is the most effective, and many people try a number of strategies for stopping smoking in vain before they find one that is suited for them. Because of this, we decided to put together a list of ten tips that can be of assistance to you in kicking the habit of smoking once and for all.

The habit of smoking cigarettes can have a negative impact not only on one's finances but also on their health. Because smoking ultimately causes death for the great majority of smokers, quitting is absolutely necessary for anyone who wants to live a longer life and spend less money over the course of their lifetime. If you've tried to quit smoking in the past but were unable to do so, the 10 tips that are provided in the following paragraphs can assist you in successfully kicking the habit this time.

The majority of people find that giving up smoking is a difficult task to accomplish. The majority of people who try to quit smoking are unsuccessful on their first attempt, and roughly eighty percent of people who are successful in quitting will start smoking again within a year of their last puff [1]. The majority of people who try to quit smoking are failed on their first attempt. On the other hand, it is crucial that you are aware that there are things you can do to make giving up smoking easier and to boost your chances of being successful in doing so. [2] If you've decided that it's time to stop the habit once and for all, read on for some helpful advice that can get you there.

Quitting smoking is a process that may be quite difficult, and as a result, you may find that you are inclined to give up before you have even started the process. On the other hand, if you are able to keep your resolution and follow these ten ideas to quit smoking for good, you will find that the procedure is considerably less difficult than you would have thought it to be. If you wish to put an end to your smoking habit once and for all, the single most crucial thing to bear in mind is that there is no one method that is certain to be successful. You need to experiment with different approaches until you find one that works well for you, and then you should stick with that approach.

Some smokers might think that the concept of quitting smoking "a little at a time" is straightforward and uncomplicated, but in actuality, this method can be challenging and even cruel to follow through with. This strategy, which is often referred to as the "reduction" technique, entails gradually cutting down on the amount of cigarettes smoked on a daily basis up until the point where the smoker is able to quit smoking altogether.

The difficulty with using this approach is that it is not an efficient technique to kick the habit of smoking. Cutting back on the amount of cigarettes smoked on a daily basis might cause withdrawal symptoms to last for a longer period of time, which can make quitting smoking an even more difficult task in the long term. Additionally, it demands a significant amount of support and encouragement from friends or family members, who will need to chat to the smoker on a daily basis and pretend to be encouraging, despite the fact that they dislike the smoker.

In addition, the strategy may be hard on the smoker's mental and physical well-being. Complaining is likely to begin when the smoker has reduced their daily cigarette consumption to 30 out of 40. The smoker will be in a state of moderate abstinence by the time they reach the third week, and by the time they reach the end of the first month, they will be in a state of significant cancellation. However, by the time they reach the 30th to the 39th day, they will have reached the most severe stage of withdrawal, during which they will be in excruciating pain and have nothing to show for their efforts.

One of the most significant drawbacks of this approach is the potential for it to result in relapse. The smoker will be in chronic abstinence after weeks or months of reducing the amount of cigarettes smoked, during which time they will be denying themselves 35–40 cigarettes on a daily basis; nonetheless, they will not be any closer to stopping smoking than the day they began the process. Furthermore, if the person who smokes is told that if things become tough, they may just take a hit every now and then to help them get through it, they will remain smoke-free for the rest of their lives.

In comparison, going cold turkey can be challenging but is not impossible to accomplish. The withdrawal symptoms will start to fade away after a period of three days. On the other hand, the severity of the withdrawal symptoms will continue to increase over the course of weeks, months, or even years if you cut back on the quantity of cigarettes you smoke.

In conclusion, giving up smoking is a journey that is unique to each individual, and it is essential to identify the way that is successful for them. The strategy of gradual detachment, often known as the "a little at a time" method, may not be the most effective method for quitting smoking because it can be stressful on both the mental and physical levels and can result in relapse. Instead, it is critical to have a conversation with your healthcare physician about the method that would work best for you and to formulate a strategy before you quit smoking. It is important to keep in mind that quitting smoking is a process that demands patience and determination, but the rewards for your health and well-being will make the effort more than worthwhile.

Step Five: Get On With It!

You are now completely equipped and ready for the 'stop-date' that is written in your calendar. You have been smoking cigarettes for a few weeks now, and each time you have done so, you have glanced at the cigarette and reminded yourself that this phase of your life is coming to an end. You have given some thought to the bad consequences smoking has on one's health, and you have also given some thought to the money that you are figuratively flushing down the toilet each time you light up and feed this completely unneeded and harmful addiction. You have conducted a lot of research and read a lot of background material pertaining to smoking. In addition, you have prepared encouraging posters and posted them all about your home. As a result, you now glance at them frequently and take in the information that they provide. Now that you have the appropriate quantity and dosage of NRT, you are finally prepared to make the transition from a smoker who is addicted to cigarettes to a citizen who does not use tobacco products.

You will notice that your level of anxiety is increasing as the 'stop-date' draws closer. Concerns like, "How am I going to deal with this?" "Can I really function without having to puff on a cigarette?" "What if I give in completely?" "How am I going to make it through each day without smoking?" "What are some strategies that I can use to combat the urges?" You may feel as though you are about to give up a reliable crutch that you have depended on for many years, but the reality is that this crutch has not kept you up in strength; rather, it has only served to weaken and betray you, and you will soon be free of this shadowy passenger for good. All of these thoughts and worries are natural, given that you have the impression that you are now giving up a reliable crutch that you have relied upon for many years. Maintain your strength, and know that you have done everything that lay within your power to vanquish this demon at this point.

Make sure that both your home and your vehicle are completely clear of any items that are associated with smoking, like as ashtrays, lighters, papers, and filters. Never, ever, ever give in to the urge to save any cigarettes or tobacco "just in case"; the risk of giving in to this temptation is simply too high, and doing so will automatically sentence you to failure. If you employ this strategy, it is possible that you might have saved yourself a lot of time and effort by skipping the steps that came before it. Recognize that once you have stopped, there is no turning back. There is no turning back. You have been transferred to the NRT at this time. Carry only the minimum number of cigarettes required to see you through to the specified cutoff time. After that point, if you still have any cigarettes in your possession, you should either shred them and flush them down the toilet or put them in a trash can that is located outside of your home.

As the time draws near, it is important that you review the information "smoking-pack" that you have prepared, that you give yourself some time to relax, and that you give serious thought to the significant and positive move that you are about to do. You should keep smoking as you normally would, but when the final countdown begins, perhaps with ten or fifteen minutes left, you should give yourself permission to chain smoke if you feel the need to. I've discovered that performing this action in front of a mirror or another reflected surface, such as a window pane, is an excellent way to ingrain a potent mental image into one's consciousness. This serves as a potent reminder of how odd and absurd the habit of smoking actually is, and it gives mental ammo for when the time comes and you feel the desire to smoke — remember this revolting vision of yourself, and you will swiftly ponder whether or not you should smoke.

When the clock strikes and you put out the stub of your very last cigarette, you should take some time to celebrate and be happy. Think about this new phase of your life, one in which you are no longer enslaved by the habit of smoking. Ignore any concerns that could come up now that you've finished the last part of the process and are officially a non-smoker. Congratulations! Now, all that is required of you is to keep this position, to take things one day at a time, and to remain secure in the fact that you are making progress. There will probably be occasions when you think it is impossible and are tempted to go buy some cigarettes or maybe just take one draw. Whatever you do, DO NOT GIVE IN TO THIS TEMPTATION! There may be times when you think it is impossible, and you will be tempted to go buy some cigarettes. Willpower and the ability to maintain a strong character are going to come in handy at this point. Utilize all of your available resources, such as your "smoking pack," the posters that are up on the walls, the memory you have of when you had your very last cigarette, as well as your support network of friends and family.

The nicotine replacement therapy (NRT) is going to be your best friend during these first few days of quitting smoking. If you maintain the correct dosage and techniques of usage, this will be of tremendous assistance to you in minimizing any desires to the barest minimum. If you are going to use microtabs, make sure you get enough. During the first few days of quitting smoking, you need to make sure that there is always enough nicotine in your system, but you shouldn't go above the suggested dosage. You will rapidly discover that as each day passes, your body will automatically begin to minimize the quantity of microtabs that are required of you. The same is true with the nicotine inhalator; make use of it whenever you feel that the urges to smoke are getting too overwhelming (despite the use of microtabs), and all you need to do is put something to your lips, take a deep breath, and feel the sensation of nicotine entering your lungs. Carry it with you wherever you go for the first few weeks, and use it as an appropriate replacement for a cigarette in situations where you would normally smoke one, such as when you take a break from work to smoke cigarettes or other similar situations.

Treat yourself with kindness. You are now battling one of the most powerful chemical addictions known to man, and the road ahead of you is not going to be an easy one. Mark in large letters on your calendar each day that you make it through without smoking, and take some time every so often to evaluate how far you've come. Calculate how much money you are saving as each day, week, and ultimately the months roll by without smoking, and refer back to the list of things you wanted to buy but could never afford to because of your addiction. As each day, week, and eventually the months roll by without smoking, calculate how much money you are saving.

It is important to remember to take things one day at a time, to periodically congratulate yourself, and to keep your supportive friends informed. As more and more days go by in which you don't smoke, you should keep track of the amount of money you save and be aware of the ways in which your health is getting better. Keep an optimistic attitude! Keep using your NRT as directed for about a month, and then slowly wean yourself off of it until you no longer need it. Be unwavering in your convictions and show some guts. You are able to, and will, achieve success! Believe in yourself and exhibit self-assurance. I hope that this phase in your life will be a lovely and pleasant experience for you, and I wish you the best of luck and strength. It is without a doubt one of the best decisions I have ever made in my whole life.

The Adverse Impacts Of Cigarette Use On The Individual

The primary cause of cellular breakdown in the lungs is smoking, which is also linked to several types of cancerous development, including those of the throat, mouth, bladder, and pancreas. Quitting smoking is the single most effective step one can do to reduce their risk of developing a disease and protect their body from additional damage. In addition, it is critical to have routine illness screenings, particularly in the event that you come from a family with a history of cancer or in the event that you are at a high risk for developing disease yourself.

Issues with one's breathing

Tobacco smoking is linked to a variety of respiratory diseases and conditions, including chronic bronchitis, emphysema, and chronic obstructive pneumonic disease (COPD). Tobacco smoke contains dangerous synthetic substances that cause damage to the lining of the airways and the lungs, making it more difficult to breathe and increasing the risk of contracting a disease. Quitting smoking is the most effective approach to prevent future damage to the lungs and put an end to the respiratory problems that have been plaguing you. In addition, practicing good respiratory hygiene, such as covering one's mouth and nose while hacking or sniffling, cleaning one's surroundings on a constant basis, and avoiding exposure to toxins and allergens, can be helpful in the process of improving one's respiratory health.

Diseases of the Heart and Blood Vessels

The use of tobacco products is one of the most important risk factors for cardiovascular disease, the most common types of which being coronary heart disease, stroke, and peripheral arterial disease. Quitting smoking is the most important measure you can take to reduce your risk of developing cardiovascular disease. In addition, adopting a healthy lifestyle that includes regular physical activity, a balanced diet, and stress management can help in the process of improving cardiovascular health.

a compromised immunological response

When a person smokes, their immune system can weaken, making it more difficult for their body to battle off infections and diseases. Putting an end to one's smoking habit is the best approach to protect one's immune system from suffering more damage and is the most effective way to restore a weakened immune system. In addition, maintaining a high standard of hygiene, receiving an adequate amount of rest, and adopting a healthy way of life can all contribute to the continued development of resistant framework capabilities.

Consequences detrimental to the pregnancy

When a woman smokes while she is pregnant, she increases her risk of having an unsuccessful labor, an early birth, a low birth weight, and various other complications. Quitting smoking either before becoming pregnant or while pregnant is essential in order to avoid the negative effects that smoking has on pregnancy. In addition, getting prenatal care, adopting a healthy lifestyle, and avoiding exposure to secondhand cigarette smoke are all things that can assist with further developing pregnancy results.

METHODS AND TECHNIQUES FOR QUITTING SMOKING

The majority of people who smoke have, at some point in their life, entertained the idea of giving up the habit. However, the sensations of wanting to give up disappear almost immediately as they appear. We all have a natural inclination to divert our attention away from things that are stressful or challenging for us. On the other hand, given that nicotine is more addictive than crack cocaine, it's not hard to understand why smokers have such a hard time giving up the habit. In addition to this, the manufacturers of cigarettes add hundreds of other compounds, some of which amplify the addictive properties. However, a smoker does have a number of options and strategies at their disposal with which to fight back and prevail. There is a wealth of information available on how to quit smoking, as well as a variety of products and strategies that are highly effective.

Make a well-thought-out plan for your time spent smoking, and set a specific quit date in your mind for when you will no longer light up. Many people believe that quitting smoking should be celebrated as a momentous occasion. If you make a big deal out of quitting smoking, you will provide yourself with the additional push that you need to quit smoking for good. Having a date set for when you will stop smoking is useful since it will give you time to plan things out. In addition to providing support, your physician may also be aware of additional options that you are not currently aware of. You have to be aware of the fact that you have to encircle yourself with as much support as you possibly can. It is important to remember that every action you do that moves you closer to achieving your goals will make a difference. Therefore, you should get yourself ready, establish a plan, decide on a date, and then put your plan into action.

Finding something to occupy your hands is a challenging component of kicking the habit of smoking, which is itself a challenge in and of itself. Driving has a tendency to bring out the strongest feelings. Because of this, being in a car may cause you to be reminded of previous smoking triggers, which you should try to avoid. When you have this sensation when you're driving, make sure to bring something with you that can keep your hands occupied. This piece of advice may come across as humorous, but it is actually quite useful for breaking free of this pattern of emotions. Additionally, it will prevent you from having the need to smoke.

You can discover a lot of support groups on the internet as well as in real life, and that's exactly what you need to help you through the times when things are very challenging. The state provides several 800 numbers for people who want to quit smoking so they can receive support. Because of the exorbitantly high medical expenditures associated with smoking-related illnesses, etc., it is in the best interest of every state to assist people in giving up smoking. If you do not have relatives or friends who will be there for you when you need them, then you should check in the phone directory. You won't have any trouble locating these numbers, and if you do, you always have the option of using a search engine like Google.

What goes through your head in the moments before you finally kick the habit is a significant contributor to the challenge of quitting smoking. Before you really resign, you will experience a significant increase in tension, which will make things far more challenging.

If you are serious about giving up smoking, you will treat this momentous occasion with the respect it deserves. This includes conducting the appropriate research, consulting with your primary care physician, and developing a strategy before you smoke your last cigarette. If you plan everything out in advance, you will significantly increase your chances of being successful.

Taking Charge Of Your Quitting Process Through The Use Of Self-Hypnosis

Have you ever fantasized of being able to modify your own thoughts and actions on your own, without needing the assistance of anybody else? If that's the case, you are going to like what we have in store for you in the following chapter. Self-hypnosis is a very effective method that empowers you to take charge of the process of quitting smoking and gives you the opportunity to make profound changes in your life, beginning from the core outward. Why is it so vital to learn about self-hypnosis when you are embarking on a path to give up smoking? Self-hypnosis makes it possible for you to be the architect of your own change; hence, you won't have to rely on the assistance of any third party in order to accomplish the objectives you set for yourself.

In order to have a handle on how self-hypnosis works, we need to first get a handle on how hypnosis works in general. In earlier chapters, we covered topics such as the scientific rationale underlying hypnosis (Chapter 3), as well as the connection between meditation and hypnosis (Chapter 4). You may recall that hypnosis is a condition characterized by intense concentration as well as relaxation in which the subconscious mind is more open to receiving ideas. When we are in this state, we are more receptive to hypnotic suggestions, which might help us change habits such as giving up smoking (Chapter 6). But how exactly can we put these suggestions into practice on our own with the help of self-hypnosis?

The practice of self-hypnosis involves inducing a hypnotic state on oneself and then feeding that hypnotic state the suggestions that one wishes to implant in one's subconcious mind. Self-hypnosis can be useful for a wide range of purposes. You will learn, as your familiarity with self-hypnosis techniques grows, that you do not require the assistance of a hypnotist to enter a condition in which you are deeply focused while still being completely relaxed.

In point of fact, many successful people all over the world have turned to self-hypnosis in order to overcome a broad variety of issues, ranging from the fear of public speaking to the inability to lose weight. Self-hypnosis gives you the capacity to modify and adapt recommendations to meet your unique requirements, which can considerably boost the success of your efforts to give up smoking. This is one of the most major advantages of self-hypnosis, and it's also one of its most useful applications.

What are your thoughts on the possibility of utilizing self-hypnosis as a method for kicking the habit of smoking? Do you believe that you could benefit from learning how to direct your mind into a state of profound attention and relaxation, and that you could then benefit from receiving individualized suggestions to help you overcome your addiction to tobacco? If you are interested in gaining additional knowledge, we encourage you to continue reading this chapter. Here, we will go into particular self-hypnosis techniques and investigate how you might use them to take charge of the process of quitting smoking. If you are keen to learn more, we urge you to continue reading this chapter.

It is time to delve into the specific techniques of self-hypnosis and see how they might be employed in the process of quitting smoking now that you have a general understanding of how self-hypnosis operates and how it functions.

Experts in the field of hypnosis have created and perfected a variety of techniques that can be used for self-hypnosis over the course of many years. Self-hypnosis has been shown to be beneficial in the treatment of a variety of ailments and issues, such as the management of pain (Patterson & Jensen, 2003), the management of stress (Waxman, 1989), and, of course, the management of smoking cessation (Barnes, Dong, McRobbie, Walker, & Mehta, 2010). Several studies and authors have supported the usefulness of self-hypnosis in the treatment of various conditions and issues.

In the 1930s, American physician and psychologist Edmund Jacobson devised a method known as "Jacobson's progressive relaxation," which is now widely used as a self-hypnosis technique. Jacobson made the groundbreaking discovery that tension in our muscles and in our thoughts are frequently intertwined. This means that if we relax our muscles, we may also relax our minds. The technique of progressive relaxation developed by Jacobson involves gradually contracting and then releasing a variety of muscle groups, beginning with the toes and working one's way up to the head. You can learn to identify and release tension in your body by practicing this technique. This will help you to attain a level of profound relaxation that is conducive to self-hypnosis, which will allow you to more easily access your subconscious mind.

One further method of self-hypnosis that is commonly employed is called "guided imagery," in which you imagine being in a peaceful and soothing setting for yourself. Because it helps to quiet the mind and allows ordinary thoughts and anxieties to melt away, this approach can be very helpful for people who deal with stress and anxiety because it helps to calm the mind. Imagine being in a location that makes you feel absolutely secure, at ease, and at one with the world, like a tranquil beach or a beautiful garden. As you completely submerge yourself in this mental image, you could discover that it is much simpler to attain a state of profound relaxation and maintain your concentration.

www.ingramcontent.com/pod-product-compliance
Lightning Source LLC
Chambersburg PA
CBHW050240120526
44590CB00016B/2161